Withdrawn

# MARY · FORD

# SUGAR FLOWERS

## CAKE DECORATING

### WITH STEP-BY-STEP INSTRUCTIONS

## ACKNOWLEDGEMENTS

Mary Ford wishes to thank Ray Hovell for all the flowers he has produced in the making of this book.

## OTHER MARY FORD TITLES

101 CAKE DESIGNS
ANOTHER 101 CAKE DESIGNS
CONCISE BOOK OF CAKE MAKING AND
    DECORATING
PARTY CAKES
SUGARPASTE CAKE DECORATING
MAKING CAKES FOR MONEY
MAKING SOFT TOYS

Copyright 1990 Michael Ford and Mary Ford

Published by Mary Ford Publications Limited,
28-30 Southbourne Grove, Southbourne, Bournemouth, Dorset BH6 3RA, England.

Printed in Italy by *Arti Grafiche* V. Bona S.r.l. - Torino

ISBN 0 946429 12 X

# Contents

## AUTHOR

MARY FORD grew up in the depths of the Gloucestershire countryside and, as a child, was fascinated by the wealth of wild flowers around her. As an adult her fascination with flowers continued and she takes great pride in her own beautiful garden, and maintains a keen interest in plants of all kinds which has greatly influenced the variety of flowers selected for this book.

Her unique talent for cake artistry has enabled her to combine the two passions, producing exquisitely designed cakes with floral decoration and passing on her skills through her books.

Her husband Michael, the artistic adviser, editor and photographer for this book, even took his camera to the Amazon jungle to capture for her the exotic beauty of the orchids and others flowers he encountered in his search for lost tribes of the rain forests.

## INTRODUCTION

MARY FORD excels at delicate sugar artistry and this practical, beautifully illustrated, pictorial guide provides cake decorators with easy-to-follow instructions for making a variety of exquisitively coloured sugar flowers suitable for all types of celebration cakes. The wide selection of piped, moulded and crystallised flowers from all seasons ensures that the decorator has available superb cake embellishment for every occasion.

All the equipment required, including cutter shapes and piping tubes, is illustrated at the start of the step-by-step instructions for making individual flowers. There is a useful guide to making posies, decorated vases and realistic floral sprays, which can also be adapted for table decoration.

This book is essential reading and an invaluable source-book of ideas and techniques for everyone involved in cake-decorating.

# Introduction to Royal Icing Flowers

[Pages 12-44]

ROYAL icing flowers can be wonderfully delicate and fragile, imparting a look of airy lightness to the finished cake. They lend themselves beautifully to creating imaginative and elegant cake designs. Royal icing flowers are, however, surprisingly practical, being totally edible and completely safe for children as they require no wires. The flowers can also be made well in advance of an occasion and stored in a cardboard box until required. They can be used to decorate cakes covered in a variety of mediums such as buttercream, fondant or chocolate as well as sugar paste and royal icing, and can complement any colour scheme.

Piped royal icing can be used to create a variety of effects ranging from simple floral designs to the stylish beauty of the half relief Rose, opening up myriad possibilities for making exquisite flowers to suit every occasion. Full instructions are given for making ten beautiful piped flowers and a variety of piped floral designs.

Instructions are also given for a brushed royal icing technique which is simple to use and yet produces intricate, lacy patterns to delight the eye. And finally in the royal icing section, there is a step-by-step guide to creating an impressive Lily which, by the imaginative use of colour and shape, can be adapted to create many different effects from one basic concept.

A traditional decorating skill has also been revived featuring crystallised flower decorations which can be combined with piped royal icing leaves and stems to produce very attractive celebration cakes. This section also includes a guide to edible flowers which are suitable for crystallising throughout the seasons.

# Introduction to Flower Paste Flowers

*[Pages 45-95]*

Flower paste can be used to create exquisitely translucent, life-like flowers which range from the simple beauty of the Primrose to the exotic magnificence of the Cymbidium. The colouring can be subtle and soft-hued, or sophisticated and vibrant according to the season and the occasion. Cake designs can be delicate or dramatic, each one a unique opportunity to display the cake-decorator's own creative artistry. Flower paste flowers are an ideal embellishment for cakes of all shapes and sizes coated in sugar paste or royal icing. They are perfect for wedding cakes and can be matched to the bridal bouquet for both colour and form.

Full instructions and practical hints for using and making flower paste have been incorporated into this comprehensive section. Step-by-step techniques for moulding eleven superb flowers, beautifully photographed in full colour, and for wiring flowers into floral sprays are included, together with instructions for creating realistic leaves and foliage, and suggestions for table or place-setting ornaments made from sugar flowers.

# Mary Ford Products

THE products illustrated represent some of the tools and equipment required to complete the cakes and floral decorations in this book. All are obtainable from the Mary Ford Cake Artistry Centre or local stockists.

# Making Royal Icing

PRACTICAL HINTS

○ To ensure a good result when piping flowers, make small quantities of Royal Icing at a time.

○ Powdered albumen and water, mixed to the recipe on this page, will keep in a sealed container in the refrigerator for several days and can be used, after gently stirring, for making up Royal Icing.

○ Freshly made Royal Icing should always be used for all piped flowers.

○ Royal Icing for flowers should be firm enough to maintain a crisp shape.

○ Royal Icing should be made 24 hours before use when making run out pieces such as the Lily on p.36.

○ It is important not to add blue colouring to the Royal Icing, as is the normal practice, when beating the Royal Icing to a peak. The blue will discolour pale shades of yellow and red.

RECIPE

| | | |
|---|---|---|
| Pure Albumen Powder | 22g | ¾oz |
| Water | 140g | 5oz |
| Icing sugar (sieved) | 740g | 1lb 10oz |

MAKING ALBUMEN SOLUTION

1 Briskly stir the albumen powder into the water. Leave to dissolve for 1 hour. (Stir occasionally during this time).

2 Strain the solution into a machine bowl through muslin or a fine sieve.

MAKING ROYAL ICING

1 Stir a third of the icing sugar into albumen solution and beat for 2 minutes. Repeat until all the icing sugar is used.

2 Beat until a light, firm consistency is formed. Store in sealed container until required.

# Preparing to Pipe Flowers and Leaves

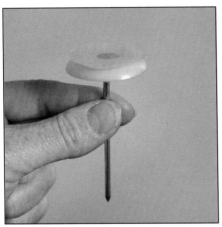

### PREPARING TO PIPE FLOWERS

*1  Cut and fix a disc of waxed paper to the top of a flower nail using royal icing. Hold the nail between finger and thumb in the position shown.*

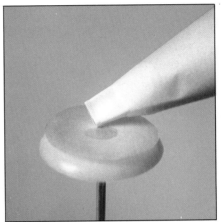

*2  Hold the piping bag, with the tube touching the waxed paper, as near to horizontal as possible. Ensure the curve of the tube is downward, thickest side at the centre. Pipe according to type of flower.*

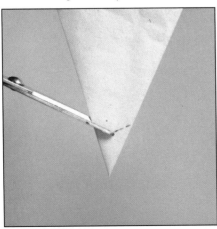

### CUTTING A LEAF BAG

*Make a greaseproof paper bag in the normal way. Cut a 'V' shape at the tip of the bag to the angle required.*

### PIPED LEAVES

*Picture shows a variety of piped leaf shapes using a 'V' cut piping bag. By varying the size of the cut, large or small leaves can be piped.*

# Violet

*T*he delicate Violet was the emblem of Napoleon Bonaparte – they reminded him of springtime in his native Corsica. Josephine wore Violets, his favourite flower, at their wedding and was given a bunch of Violets every wedding anniversary. When Napoleon was exiled to Elba, he promised to return in the Spring and his followers adopted the Violet in memory of that promise. After his death, a locket containing Violets from Josephine's grave was found around his neck.

In the language of flowers the Violet means 'I return your love' and the Parma Violet beseeches 'Let me love you'.

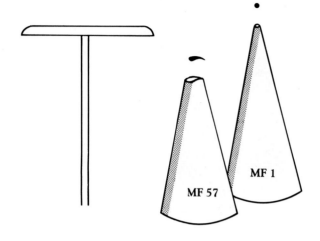

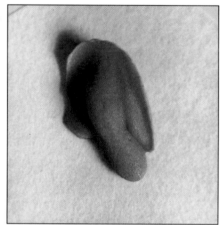

*1* Pipe a narrow petal (to the size required) on to a disc of waxed paper fixed to a flower nail. Pipe with the thicker end of the nozzle to the centre. Keep the piping bag horizontal and turn the nail slightly whilst piping the petal (MF 57).

*2* Pipe a second petal, in the same manner as in step *1*, next to the first petal joining at the side as shown.

*3* Pipe two further petals symmetrically below the completed petals to form the top of the flower head.

*4* Pipe the fifth petal to complete the violet shape as shown. Leave to dry for 1 hour.

5 Pipe in the stamens using a piping bag without a tube whilst keeping the bag upright. Leave to dry for 20 minutes.

6 Pipe in the centre of the flower (the stigma) as shown (MF 1). Leave to dry 24 hours before using for decoration.

# Narcissus

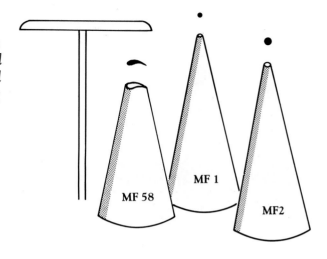

*T*he delightfully scented Narcissus blooms in the Spring. Narcissus was a beautiful Greek youth who was so much in love with himself that he would spend all day gazing at his reflection in streams and ponds. After he had spurned the love of a charming Greek maiden called Echo, who faded away, the gods turned him into the Narcissus flower so that he could stand by the water looking at his own reflection throughout eternity.

In the Chinese language of flowers the Narcissus is the symbol of good fortune and in Japan it signifies mirth and joyousness.

MF 58    MF 1    MF2

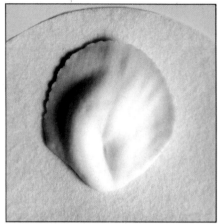

*1* Pipe a wide petal (to the size required) on to a disc of waxed paper fixed to a flower nail (MF 58). Pipe with a flowing up and down movement. Keep the piping bag horizontal and turn the nail slightly whilst piping.

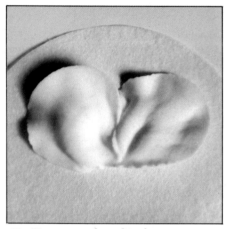

*2* Pipe a second petal in the same manner, overlapping the petals slightly to join as shown.

*3* Using the outer edge of the disc as a guide to keeping a good circular shape, pipe three further petals as shown.

*4* Complete the flower shape by piping a further petal as shown, taking care to release the pressure before gently removing the bag. Leave to dry for 1 hour.

5 Pipe a spiral line around the flower centre (MF 2) to build up the trumpet. Pipe in stamens (MF 1). Leave to dry 1 hour.

6 Overpipe the trumpet with a darker line to complete the flower (MF 1). Leave to dry for 24 hours before using for decoration.

# Apple Blossom

*A*pple Blossom has been used since ancient times to symbolise fertility, wisdom and immortality. In ancient Greece a branch of Apple Blossom was the traditional bridal offering because the apple was sacred to Aphrodite, the goddess of love.

This delicately coloured flower, which blends into many colour-schemes, is particularly suitable for wedding or anniversary cakes as, in the language of flowers, it symbolises perpetual harmony.

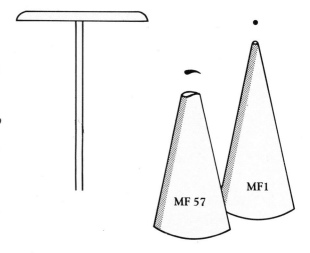

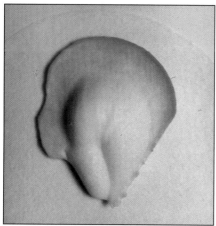

*1* Fill a piping bag with two colours of royal icing. Pipe a wide petal (to the size required) on to a disc of waxed paper fixed to a flower nail (MF 57). Keep the piping bag horizontal and turn the nail slightly whilst piping.

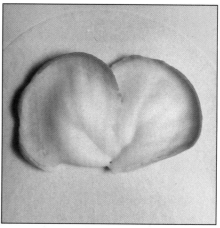

*2* Pipe a second petal, in the same manner as in step *1*, next to the first petal joining at the side as shown. Ensure that the petals are of even thickness and size.

*3* Pipe a further petal using steady pressure on the piping bag to achieve petals of a consistent size.

*4* A fourth petal should be piped as shown. Use the outer edge of the disc as a guide to placing the petals to form a circular shape.

**5** *Pipe the fifth and final petal, to complete a uniform flower shape. Leave to dry for 1 hour.*

**6** *Pipe the stamens as shown in the centre of the apple blossom, keeping the piping bag upright (MF 1). Leave to dry for 24 hours before using for decoration.*

# Daisy

*T*he Daisy is the flower of April, symbolising gentleness and innocence. Its Anglo-Saxon name Daeges Eage (Day's Eye) is derived from its habit of closing its petals at the end of the day and Chaucer tells us that he rose with the sun to watch the flower open, and knelt beside it in the evening to watch it close.

The flower goes back to Roman times however. Legend has it that a nymph, Belides, was dancing one day when she attracted the unwelcome attention of the god of the orchard. To protect herself she transformed into the humble Daisy. The latin name for the Daisy is Bellis, meaning Belides' flower.

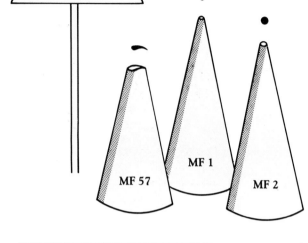

MF 57    MF 1    MF 2

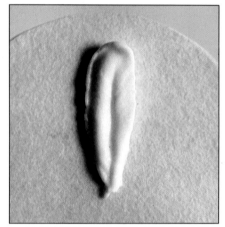

*1* Pipe a narrow upright petal (to the size required) on to a disc of waxed paper fixed to a flower nail (MF 57). Keep the piping bag horizontal and turn the nail very slightly when piping.

*2* Continue to pipe petals, working in a clockwise direction using the outer edge of the disc as a guide to the finished shape.

*3* Pipe further petals to complete the flower. Leave to dry 12 hours.

*4* Using a clean, fine and soft artists' brush, tint the outside edge with confectioners' dusting powder. (NOTE: The shade of confectioners' dusting powder can be lightened by the addition of cornflour.)

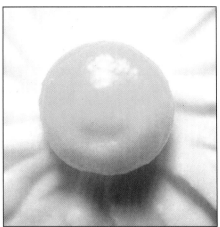

5 Pipe a bulb to form the centre of the daisy as shown (MF 2). Leave to dry 30 minutes.

6 Pipe small dots over the bulb to form the stamens (MF 1). Leave to dry 24 hours before using for decoration.

# Primrose

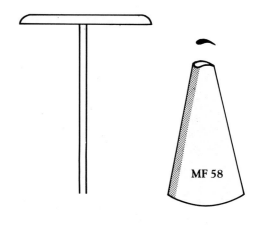

MF 58

*T*he Primrose blooms during mild spells in winter, and is one of the most delightful messengers of spring. The sunny yellow flower has darker yellow lines pointing to its centre which are known as 'honey guides' as they are supposed to lead bees to the nectar.

The Primrose is an ideal cake decoration for delicate winter or spring celebration designs. It is particularly suitable for Mother's Day cakes as, in the past, bunches of Primroses were traditionally gathered by servants returning home for Mothering Sunday.

*1* Pipe a heart-shaped petal on to a disc of waxed paper fixed to a flower nail (MF 58). To make the heart-shape, half-way through piping the petal quickly move the wrist down, and then up again in a flowing movement, keeping an even pressure, whilst turning the nail.

*2* Pipe a second petal in the same manner as step *1*, ensuring that the petals are of even thickness. Overlap slightly at the base to join the petals together.

*3* Pipe two further petals of consistent size and shape.

*4* Complete the circular shape by carefully piping a fifth petal. Release the pressure before gently lifting the bag away. Leave to dry 12 hours.

*5* Using a clean, fine and soft artists' brush, colour the broad centre with confectioners' dusting powder or edible food colouring.

*6* Colour the very centre to complete the flower. Leave to dry for 24 hours before using for decoration.

# Pansy

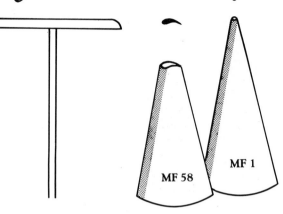

MF 58     MF 1

*T*he multi-coloured Pansy blooms continuously through the late spring and on through summer to early autumn. The Pansy was always found in cottage gardens and, in olden days, was known as 'Heartsease' as its happy smiling face was reputed to bring peace and tranquillity to the beholder. In the early 19th century Lord Gambier, discharged from the Navy under a cloud, took up gardening to forget his troubles. His gardener, Mr Thompson, was known as the Father of Heartsease as he pioneered the 'face' of the Pansy.

The gentle beauty of the Pansy is suitable for use throughout the seasons.

*1* Fill a piping bag with two colours of royal icing. Pipe a horseshoe shaped petal (to the size required) on to a disc of waxed paper fixed to a flower nail (MF 58). Keep the piping bag horizontal and turn the nail whilst piping.

*2* Pipe a second petal of the same shape and size, in the same manner as in step *1*.

*3* Maintaining a consistent pressure and shape, pipe a third petal as shown.

*4* Pipe a fourth petal to complete the upper part of the flower. The four petals should cover just over half of the waxed paper disc.

5 Complete the flower by piping a wider petal at the base. The width should equal the two top petals. Allow to dry 1 hour.

6 Paint stamens around the centre of the flower with edible food colouring. Pipe the stigma (MF 1) from the centre of the flower with a 'tail' towards the bottom petal as shown. Leave to dry for 24 hours.

# Sweet Pea

*I*n the language of flowers the Sweet Pea signifies pleasure and the beautifully coloured and scented Sweet Pea is ideal for celebration cakes for all seasons.

The Sweet Pea was introduced into England from Sicily by a monk who sent the seeds to a schoolmaster friend at the end of the 17th century. It has now almost died out in its native habitat but is being reintroduced from plants found in Quito, Ecuador, which were taken there centuries ago by the Spaniards.

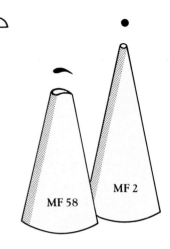

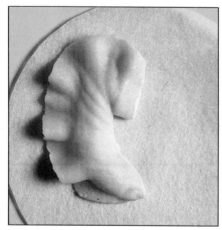

*1* With the thicker side of the piping tube towards the centre and keeping the bag horizontal, pipe outer petal (to the size required) on to a disc of waxed paper fixed to a flower nail (MF 58).

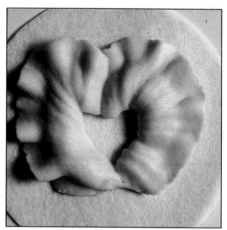

*2* Reversing the direction of the petal, pipe a second petal to form a heart shape as shown.

*3* Holding the piping bag so that the piping tube is standing away from the centre, pipe a small heart within the outer petals, forming the inner petals as shown.

*4* Holding the piping bag vertically, pipe the flower centre as shown. Leave to dry for 12 hours.

**5** Using a soft, fine and clean artists' brush, delicately colour the edges of all petals with confectioners' dusting powder or edible food colouring.

**6** Holding the piping bag horizontally, pipe the calyx at the base of the petals as shown (MF 2). Leave to dry for 24 hours before using for decoration.

# Open Rose

*T*he ancient Egyptians, Persians, Greeks and Romans all relied upon Attar of the Damask Rose as a cosmetic and a perfume to enhance their beauty. Persian legend tells us that the Caliph Jehangir was walking with his lovely bride in the palace garden when he noticed that the fountain pools, which had been filled with rose petals to celebrate their wedding, had an oily film which smelt heavenly. He ordered this to be bottled and Attar of Roses was considered to be one of the most precious of all fragrances.

The beautiful Rose can be used to decorate cakes at any time of the year.

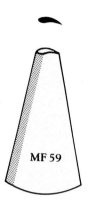

MF 59

1 Make a cone shape from almond paste to an appropriate size for the rose to be piped on.

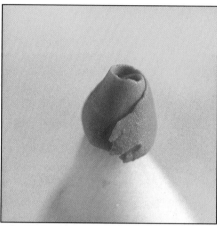

2 With steady pressure, pipe a vertical petal on the top of the cone, turning it whilst piping and finishing as shown (MF 59).

3 Holding the bag slightly away from the centre, and commencing at approximately the last quarter of the previous petal, pipe a more loosely wrapped petal which protrudes above the centre as shown.

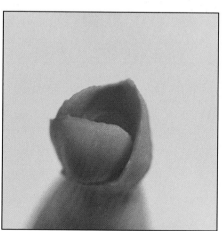

4 Pipe a further two petals around the rose centre, overlapping each petal as shown.

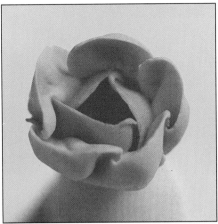

5 Continue piping petals around the outside of the rose to build up the rose shape. Leave to dry for 2 hours.

6 Pipe a row of petals around the base of the rose to complete the open shape. Leave to dry for 24 hours. Carefully remove from the cone before using as decoration.

# Rose Buds

*T*he Rosebud signifies beauty and youth. Legend says that one day Chloris, the goddess of flowers, was walking in the woods and found a beautiful nymph who had died. Chloris decided to give the nymph new life as a flower of unsurpassed beauty. She enlisted the aid of the other gods and goddesses who each added their blessing – Aphrodite gave purity of form and Dionysus (the god of wine) added a fragrant nectar. When the new flower, the Rose, was completed, it was presented by Aphrodite to her son Eros, the god of love.

Rosebuds are ideal for delicate sprays to enhance any celebratory cake.

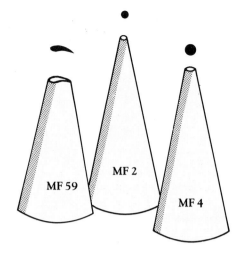

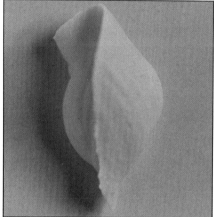

1 On a square of waxed paper, keeping the piping bag upright, pipe the central petal (to the size required) in the shape shown (MF 59).

2 Holding the piping bag upright, with the thick end at the base, pipe the right-hand petal as shown.

3 Complete the bud by piping the left-hand petal in the shape illustrated. Leave to dry for 1 hour.

4 With a leaf shaped piping bag (see page 11), pipe the calyx to form the half rose. Complete by piping the stem (MF 2). Allow to dry for 24 hours before using for decoration.

**5** For a tight bud, pipe a pear shaped or plain elongated shell to form the bud centre (MF 4). Allow to dry for 1 hour.

**6** With a leaf shaped piping bag, pipe the calyx around the bud as shown. Then pipe the stem (MF 2). Allow to dry for 24 hours before using for decoration.

# Half Relief Rose

*A*lthough Roses have been cultivated for thousands of years the garden Rose, as it is grown today, is a recent creation. In Victorian times the short-lived flowers of the English climbing Rose were crossed with the perpetual flowering Chinese Rose and the bright colours of the Persian Rose to produce the dazzling array of colours now available.

   The Rose is the most popular flower for cake decoration, no matter what the occasion. The Red Rose symbolises love and desire, the White Rose charm and innocence, whilst the Pink Rose declares 'Our love is perfect happiness'.

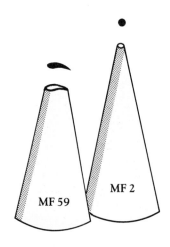

MF 59    MF 2

*1* On a square of waxed paper, keeping the piping bag upright, pipe the central petal (to the size required) in the shape shown (MF 59).

*2* Keeping the piping bag upright, pipe a second and third petal either side of the first, opening out the third petal slightly as shown.

*3* Pipe two further petals angling the piping bag to open out the rose shape.

*4* Continue to build the rose shape by piping a further petal each side as shown.

5 Complete the flower by piping two further petals as shown. Leave to dry for 1 hour.

6 Pipe the calyx around the base of the petals with a leaf shaped piping bag (see page 11), and then pipe the stem (MF 2). Leave to dry for 24 hours before using for decoration.

# Piped Floral Designs

Most of the designs illustrated below are ideal for piping on any celebration cake. By varying the size of the piped design, it can be used for decorating the side of the cake or, if required, as a main feature on top of a cake.

Piped lines to create floral shapes are very attractive on *petits fours*, chocolates, biscuits, gateaux and desserts.

Experimenting with colour, size, shape and arrangement is an inexpensive way of learning floral artistry skills and will enable the decorator to widen the variety of work presented for each occasion. Mixing flower heads with stems and leaves affords endless design possibilities.

Picture 8 illustrates a floral curve which is an ideal pattern for the side of a royal icing or sugarpaste coated wedding cake. These floral designs can be coloured to match bridesmaids' dresses or flowers for this happy occasion.

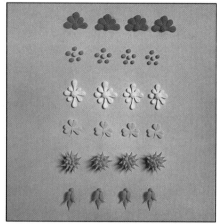

*1 A variety of piped dots, shells and spikes can be used to form floral shapes for use on most celebration cakes.*

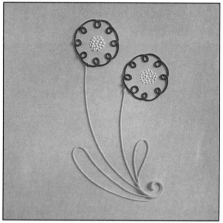

*2 Keeping the piping tube (MF 1) upright, pipe the flower head outline in one continuous movement. Pipe the centre dots. Pipe the stem and leaves to fit the shape of the cake.*

*3 Pipe the flower petals and then the heads and stamens (MF 1). Pipe the stems with a sweeping movement to give a flowing effect.*

*4 Keeping the bag upright, pipe the flower petals (MF 2), followed by the flower centres. (The nearer the tube is to the surface, the wider the petal will be.) Pipe stems and leaves as shown (MF 1).*

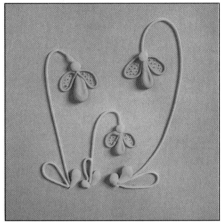

5   Pipe the flower centres (MF 2). Pipe individual petals as shown (MF 1) and then the base of each flower. Pipe the stems and leaves in the design shown.

6   Pipe two stems (MF 1) and then pipe the flowers and stamens (MF 2). Using a piping bag cut into a 'V', pipe the leaves as shown (see page 11).

7   Pipe stems in a variety of lengths (MF 1). Pipe a flower, with heart shaped petals, at the top of each stem in the design shown (MF 1). Pipe the small leaves on to the stems (MF 1). Using a 'V' cut piping bag (see page 11), pipe leaves at the base.

8   At the centre of the design, pipe a large flower in the appropriate position (MF 1). Pipe a curved line each side of the flower and then pipe flowers, buds and leaves as required.

# Brushed Embroidery

Brushed embroidery is a very simple technique and the versatile medium produces delicate patterns which can be coloured to produce dramatic or soft effects. The technique can be worked with coloured icing or white icing which can be highlighted when dry. Several colours can be blended into a design.

A wide variety of beautiful patterns and textures are possible, including lace. A very simple but effective design is illustrated below. This style of decoration is ideal for use by the natural artist.

### MATERIALS

- ○ Paper for template.
- ○ Sharp pointed tool.
- ○ Pencil.
- ○ Scissors.
- ○ Piping tubes.
- ○ Fine paint brush.
- ○ Food colouring.

### MEDIUM

3 tablespoons of royal icing can be mixed with ¼ teaspoon of clear piping jelly (if available) for all brushed royal icing work. (The icing remains workable slightly longer if piping jelly is used.)

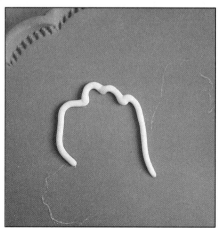

*1 Draw and cut out paper templates. Place on coated cake-top and scratch template outlines carefully into the coating. Remove the templates.*

*2 Overpipe part of the scratched petal line with royal icing.*

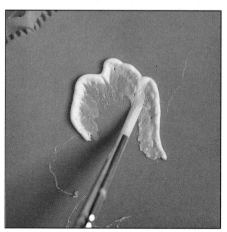

*3 Immediately brush the icing to the centre of the petal to achieve the effect shown.*

**4** Continue to work one petal at a time until the flower is completed.

**5** Pipe the leaf outline and brush to centre. Pipe the leaf veins. Complete the design by piping in the stems.

# Lily

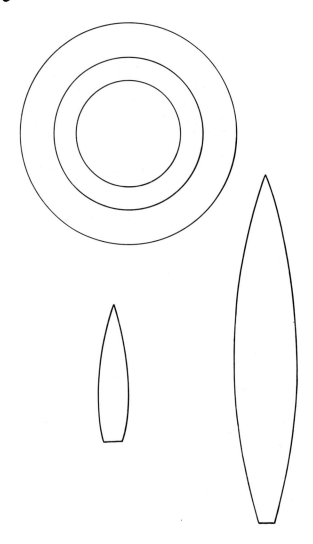

*L*ilies make an extremely attractive cake decoration and the imaginative use of shape and colour can create many different effects by slight alterations to the basic design. Lilies are particularly suitable for wedding and other celebration cakes and have traditionally been associated with Easter.

## ROYAL ICING RUNOUTS

### PRACTICAL HINTS

○ **Important note:** Only use royal icing made at least 24 hours before commencing the lily runout.
○ Glycerine should not be used in the royal icing for this work.
○ Royal icing for runouts should be made with pure albumen powder.
○ Convert royal icing for runout work by folding in sufficient cold water to achieve a dropping consistency.
○ A piped runout outline must be complete to prevent seepage.
○ Before filling a piping bag with runout royal icing, tap the container on the table to bring air bubbles to the surface.
○ Use good quality waxed paper.

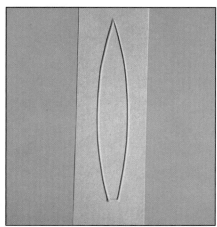

*1 Using long template under waxed paper and a fine piping tube, outline a petal with royal icing (MF 0).*

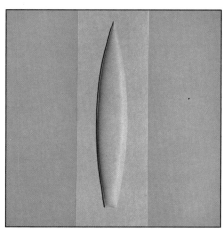

*2 Flood-in the petal with soft royal icing containing no glycerine.*

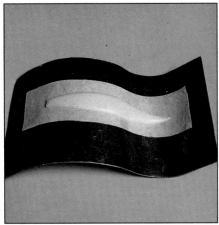

*3* Whilst the petal is still wet, place on curved piece of tin. Repeat steps *1-3* for each petal. Leave to dry for 24 hours. 6 petals are required.

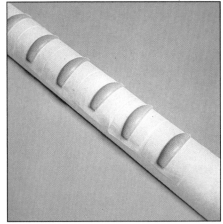

*4* Repeat steps *1-2* using short template. Place over a curved surface of appropriate size and leave to dry for 24 hours. 6 petals are required.

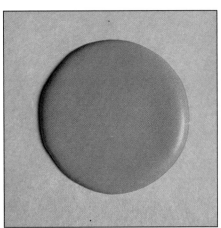

*5* Outline and flood-in on waxed paper one of each size disc using templates as a guide (MF 1).

*6* (A) Pipe a bulb on to waxed paper (MF 3). Leave to dry 2 hours. (B) Pipe spikes around the base (MF 1). Leave to dry 10 minutes. (C) Enclose bulb with spikes. Leave to dry 24 hours.

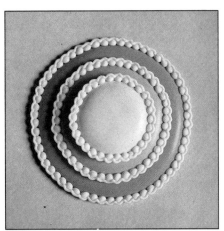

*7* Pipe bulbs around the edge of each disc. Pipe a line over each bulb (MF 0). Leave to dry 12 hours. Remove the small discs from the waxed paper and fix to large disc using royal icing.

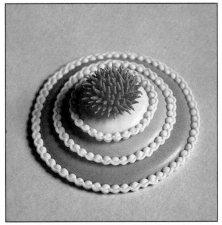

*8* Fix flower to centre of top disc.

 37

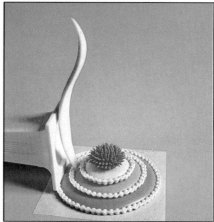

**9** *Using royal icing, fix and support one petal to the middle disc.*

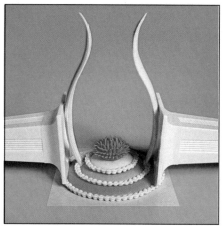

**10** *Repeat step 9 on opposite side. It is essential to ensure the petals are directly opposite each other and that they are both upright. Leave to dry 2 hours.*

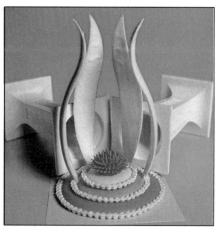

**11** *Fix and support two more petals.*

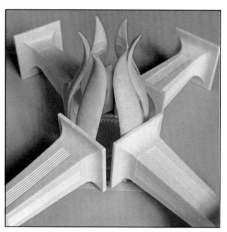

**12** *Fix and support remaining two petals. Leave to dry 12 hours before removing supports.*

**13** *Remove supports and test each petal for movement or weakness. Strengthen with royal icing if necessary.*

**14** *Fix lily onto centre of cake-top.*

**15** Fix small petals around middle disc as shown.

**16** Decorate with matching flowers at base of large petals.

(a)

(c)

(d)

(e)

(f)

(b)

(g)

(k)

(l)

(m)

(n)

(o)

(r)

(i)

(j)

(p)  (q)

# Crystallised Flowers

CRYSTALLISED flowers are traditional decorations which are extremely easy to make and most attractive in appearance.

Flowers should be carefully selected to ensure that they are edible. Flowers from a bulb, such as daffodils, snowdrops or lily of the valley, should never be used. The beautiful blue borage flower has a wonderful colour and taste, as do rose petals, violets and nasturtiums. Most fruit-tree blossoms and some shrubs, such as mimosa or japonica, are also suitable for crystallising.

A fine selection of edible flowers are illustrated on page 40.

Flowers should be picked when they have just opened, preferably at mid-day when they are completely dry and free from insects. Ensure that the chosen flowers have not been sprayed with insecticide. Discard any which are not perfectly formed or which are shrivelled or blemished. Crystallised flowers can be prepared when the blossom is in season as they will keep for several months if stored between layers of tissue paper in an airtight tin. The finished flowers can make an attractive winter decoration for cakes as well as place or table settings, at a time when fresh flowers are difficult to find.

---

**CRYSTALLISING THROUGH THE SEASONS**
Flowers in ( ) are pictured on page 40.

| SPRING | Hibiscus |
|---|---|
| Almond Blossom | Honeysuckle (d) |
| Apple Blossom | Hyssop |
| Chamomile | Jasmine |
| Cherry Blossom | Lavender (b) |
| Daisy (m) | Lime Blossom |
| Heartsease | Marigold (h) |
| Honeysuckle (d) | Mimosa |
| Japonica | Nasturtium (k) |
| Lemon Balm | Passionflower (r) |
| Marjoram (q) | Pink (l) |
| Mint (e) | Rose (p) |
| Parsley (a) | Rosemary (c) |
| Primrose | Scented leaf Pelargonium |
| Sage (g) | |
| Violet | AUTUMN |
| | Clove Pink |
| SUMMER | Nasturtium (k) |
| Borage | Pansy (f) |
| Carnation (i) | Single Chrysanthemum |
| Chive (o) | |
| Cornflower (j) | WINTER |
| Dandelion (n) | Jasmine |
| Evening Primrose | |

When decorating cakes with crystallised flowers, they can look very attractive arranged in a bunch and individual flowers can be combined with piped royal icing leaves and stems.

MARY picked jasmine and roses from her garden to illustrate how the delicate beauty of flowers can be preserved by crystallising. The finished spray is ideal for decorating a summer wedding, or other celebration cake. The flowers can be stored until required in an airtight tin between layers of tissue paper.

| ITEMS REQUIRED |
| --- |
| ○ Freshly picked edible flowers |
| ○ Lightly beaten egg white |
| ○ Caster sugar |
| ○ Greaseproof paper |
| ○ Medium size paintbrush |
| ○ Wire tray |

*1 Carefully select suitable, edible flowers. They should be crystallised within 1 hour of picking. Ensure that flowers have not been sprayed with insecticide.*

*2 Thoroughly mix 2 teaspoons of cold water with 1 fresh egg white in a clean, grease free bowl.*

*3 Using a soft, medium-sized paintbrush, gently cover the top surface of the flower petals with egg white.*

*4 Sprinkle the flower with caster sugar and gently shake off any excess. (NOTE: the sugar can be coloured with confectioners' dusting powder or edible food colouring to match the flower if desired).*

5 Using the brush, coat the back of the petals, calyx and stem with egg white. Sprinkle with caster sugar and shake off excess. Place on greaseproof paper on a wire tray for 24 hours to crystallise.

6 Leaves can also be crystallised using steps *1-5*. Large flowers and roses should be wired around the stem and dried upside down to avoid distortion.

*1* Edible flowers, such as the Japonica illustrated, make a very attractive decoration.

*2* Crystallise the sprays using the step-by-step guide on the previous page and allow to dry completely before using for decoration.

# Flower Paste

FLOWER paste is a firm, sweet paste, generally used for modelling hand-made cake artistry flowers. The flowers can be used individually or wired together as sprays to decorate sugarpaste coated or royal iced cakes.

The design and colour of a celebration cake are extremely important factors in their appeal, and these can be greatly enhanced by the selection of appropriate flowers. When using vibrant or dark colours, only the smallest flowers should be in the darkest tones otherwise the flowers will appear to be too heavy for the cake. The larger flowers should be pale in tone and complement the overall cake colouring. The colour and type of flowers used for decoration can be linked both to the type of celebration and to the season. Light greens and yellows are springlike, as are daffodils, primroses and violets. Roses, which can be in a wide variety of colours, are linked both to the summer and to weddings. Autumnal cakes can feature chrysanthemums or the deep golden tones of falling leaves. White or blue flowers will reflect the cool shades of winter, which may be brightened by the use of exotic and colourful flowers such as the orchid.

All the flowers in this section of the book have been made using the flower paste recipe overleaf.

## TO USE FLOWER PASTE

Cut off a walnut-sized piece and knead until pliable. The warmth of your hands will bring the paste to an elastic consistency. If the paste is too stiff, add a smear of white fat and a little egg white to it. Flower paste dries out very quickly and therefore should be kept covered at all times. Only a small piece should be cut at a time as it rolls out very thinly and it is not possible to work on more than a few petals at a time (see page 48).

Care should be taken when colouring the flower paste as certain colours may affect the consistency, particularly reds and violet; and colours such as yellows and reds may deepen on standing. Always colour the paste slightly lighter than required if using red or yellow. Add extra cornflour if the consistency becomes too soft.

Flower paste should be fixed to flower paste with egg white or gum arabic solution.

---

### GUM ARABIC SOLUTION

*1* *Boil 3 ozs of water. Remove from heat and immediately whisk in 1 oz of gum arabic powder.*

*2* *Leave to cool.*

*3* *Remove any surface film and store in a refrigerator until required.*

---

## PRACTICAL HINTS

○ Work with a small quantity of flower paste as it dries out quickly once it has been rolled out and cut. Keep unused portion of flower paste in a polythene bag in the fridge until required.

○ Warmth will affect the consistency of flower paste. If you have warm hands, or if the weather is warm, a slightly stiffer consistency will be required. If you have cold hands, use a slightly softer consistency.

○ Flower paste should be coloured with edible paste colouring as liquid will affect the consistency of the paste. Colour should be added gradually using the end of a clean cocktail stick.

○ Care should be taken when colouring flower paste as some colours can affect the consistency, and red and yellow colours can deepen when left to stand.

○ Flower paste should be chilled after colouring to return it to a workable consistency as it becomes stringy with handling.

○ Flowers can be coloured with confectioners' dusting powder. When using powder, ensure that the cake is covered to prevent discolouration by powder particles in the air.

○ Thinly rolled flower paste should be used to achieve the most natural looking, translucent petals. Roll out the paste on lightly dredged cornflour or a thin layer of white fat to prevent sticking.

○ To prevent petal edges from becoming ragged, apply sufficient pressure to the cutter to cut out cleanly. With cutter upside down, gently push the petal out after running your finger around the cutter's edge.

○ A cardboard template can be used instead of a cutter if only a few flowers are required. Place the template on to the rolled out paste and carefully cut around the template using a sharp knife.

○ Work from a sample of the flower to be copied, particularly if it is the first time you have made it. If the fresh flower cannot be obtained a fabric flower can be used. Fabric flowers are also useful for practising making up sprays.

○ Wires should never be inserted directly into a cake. A small ball of sugar paste can be used to secure the spray to the cake surface, or a posy stick can be inserted into the cake.

# Making Flower Paste

| FLOWER PASTE RECIPE | | | |
|---|---|---|---|
| Cornflour | 60g | 2oz | ½ cup |
| Icing Sugar (Sieved) | 400g | 14oz | 3½ cups |
| Gum Tragacanth | 20g | ¾oz | 1 tblspn |
| Glucose Syrup | 20g | ¾oz | 1 tblspn |
| Cold Water | 60g | 2oz | 3 tblspn |
| White Fat | 20g | ¾oz | 1 tblspn |

*1 Weigh all ingredients carefully and place the icing sugar, cornflour and gum tragacanth on greaseproof paper. Tip the dry ingredients through a sieve into a bowl (sieve three times).*

*2 Add remaining ingredients into the bowl. Thoroughly mix the ingredients (on a 'slow' machine or by hand with a wooden spoon).*

*3 The paste is properly mixed when it does not stick to the side of the bowl.*

*4 Mould the paste into a ball, place into a polythene bag and leave to mature for at least 24 hours.*

# Rolling Out Flower Paste

FLOWER paste can be rolled out in a variety of ways and it should always be rolled out as thinly as possible. The methods demonstrated below are particularly recommended for pieces which are to be cut for frilling or moulding. Frilled pieces should be used and shaped immediately after completing the frill. Pieces cut for moulding can be stored between layers of polythene in a cool place.

When rolling out onto cornflour roll out very small pieces at a time as the cornflour will be absorbed into the paste, which will become stiffer each time the rolling out is repeated.

Unused flower paste should be stored in a polythene bag in the refrigerator.

## FRILLING

*1 Roll out as thinly as possible a small piece of flower paste on to a cornflour dusted surface.*

*2 Cut out the shape required using the appropriate cutter. Gently move the cut shape to ensure that it is not stuck to the work surface. Roll a cocktail stick backwards and forwards to frill the edge as shown. Dust off any surplus cornflour.*

## MOULDING

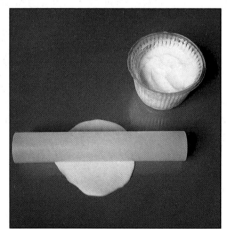

*1 Lightly grease the work surface with a small amount of white fat. Thinly roll out a small piece of flower paste over the greased area.*

*2 Cut out the shape required and lift the flower paste from the work surface using a flat, sharp knife. Press the flower paste between the finger and thumb to create a thin, clean edge.*

# Flower Paste Leaves

THERE are many varieties of leaf cutter available on the market today and an appropriate leaf shape should be selected for the flower being made.

Thinly roll out the flower paste on to a greased or cornflour dusted work surface, and vein with a mould if required. Cut to shape using the appropriate cutter. Cut a length of 24 or 28 gauge wire, moisten with egg white and insert into the centre of the leaf, keeping an even amount of flower paste each side of the wire. Leaves can be coloured with liquid, paste or powder colours.

# Daffodil

*T*he daffodil is often called the Lent Lily, and early English names were Affodyl and Daffadowndyllyes. Its bright yellow trumpets herald the arrival of spring in early March and April, making it particularly appropriate for decorating Easter, Wedding and other celebration cakes.

　　To dream of daffodils signifies a long and happy future.

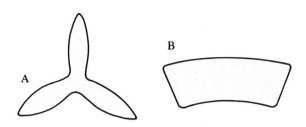

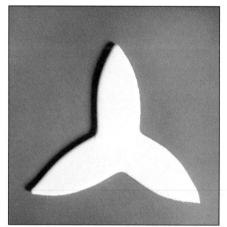

*1 Roll out and cut a petal shape from a sheet of flower paste using a cutter in the shape of **A**.*

*2 Place the petal shape on a dry household sponge and then thin the edges by gentle pressure with a ball-shaped modelling tool.*

*3 Immediately mark each petal with a cocktail stick, starting from centre to outer edges, as shown. Repeat steps **1-3** to make a second set of petals.*

*4 Moisten the centre of one of the sets of petals with egg white and immediately join the two shapes together. Pierce the centre with a cocktail stick to make a hole for the stem.*

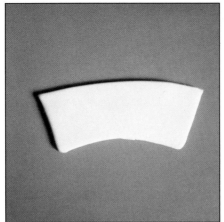

**5** *Roll out a sheet of flower paste and cut with a cutter in the shape of **B**.*

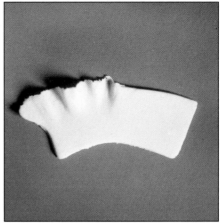

**6** *Frill the longer (outer) edge by rolling a cocktail stick backwards and forwards a little at a time.*

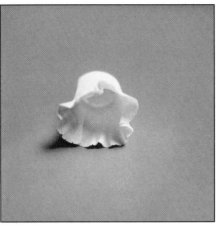

**7** *Moisten one end of the shape, then fold over and fix one end to the other to form the trumpet.*

**8** *Moisten the base of the trumpet and fix to the petals, as shown. Leave to dry for 24 hours.*

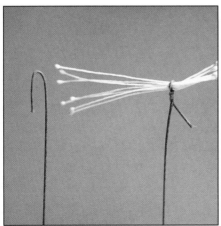

**9** *(A) Cut and bend (to shape shown) a length of lime green 24 gauge wire, to form the stem. (B) Loop seven single stamens through the wire stem and twist the stem to secure them.*

**10** *(A) Cut off stamen heads on one end and turn to the upright position. (B) Tape stamen heads to the stem with floral tape.*

**11** Mould a ball of flower paste. Moisten the tape at the base of the stamens and insert the stem through the ball of flower paste, as shown.

**12** Moisten the inside centre of the flower and insert the stem through the existing hole. Pull the stem through the flower until the flower paste ball and stamen heads are in the position shown.

**13** Use a cocktail stick to flatten the flower paste ball.

**14** Mould a cone of flower paste and insert the stem through its centre.

**15** Moisten the base of the flower and fix the cone to it, as shown. Leave to dry for 24 hours.

**16** Using a clean, soft artist's brush colour flower base with confectioners' dusting powder.

**17** *Wind floral tape around stem, leaving the top end loose. Cut loose end of tape to leaf shape. Brush leaf with confectioners' dusting powder as shown.*

**18** *Highlight the petal and trumpet edges with confectioners' dusting powder.*

# Sweet Pea

The wide variety in colour of this attractive flower make it particularly suitable for decorating cakes to harmonise with an overall colour scheme.

This plant was fashionable in Edwardian times and was a great favourite of Queen Alexandra. Nowadays there is fierce competition among enthusiastic growers to produce a prize exhibit at the ever popular flower show. The Sweet Pea is ideal for making up into sprays.

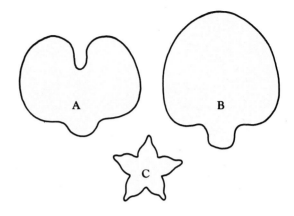

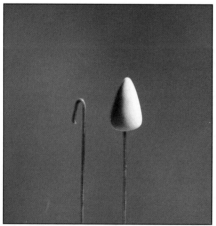

*1* (A) Cut and bend (to shape shown) a length of lime green 28 gauge wire. (B) Mould a piece of flower paste to form a cone. Moisten the end of the wire with egg white or gum arabic solution and insert into the cone.

*2* (A) Mould the base of the cone to the shape shown. (B) Pinch one side to form shape shown (which becomes the centre of the flower).

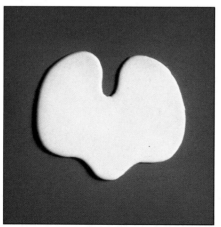

*3* Roll out and cut the petal shape shown from a sheet of flower paste using a cutter in the shape of **A**.

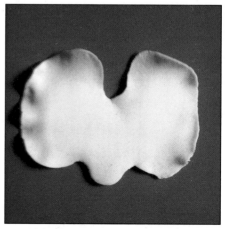

*4* Place the shape on to a dry household sponge and then thin the edge by gentle pressure with a ball-shaped tool.

*5* Moisten the centre of the petal and fix it around the flower centre. (This, with the addition of the calyx – see step *11* – completes the sweet pea bud.)

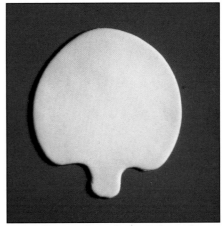

*6* Roll out and cut the petal shape shown from a sheet of flower paste using a cutter in the shape of **B**.

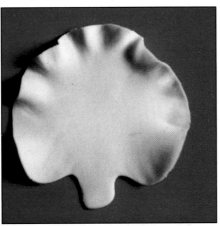

*7* Frill the edge of the petal by rolling a cocktail stick backwards and forwards a little at a time.

*8* Immediately moisten and fix the second petal to the flower head by gently curving it from behind. Pinch the centre 'tongue' (at the base of the petal) on to the wire stem. Leave to dry for 48 hours.

*9* Using a clean, soft artist's brush, highlight the flower centre and petal edges (front and back) with confectioners' dusting powder. (NOTE: The shade of confectioners' dusting powder can be lightened by the addition of cornflour).

*10* Highlight (in green confectioners' dusting powder) the base of the petals at junction with stem as shown.

*11* Using a cutter in the shape of **C**, cut the flower calyx from a sheet of flower paste.

*12* Pinch the edges of the calyx, moisten its centre then fix to the base of the flower by pushing the wire stem through the centre. Tendrils are made by twisting wire around a pencil.

# Cymbidium

*T*he Cymbidium is one of the most popular of the Orchid family and is native to Asia and Australia. It has a variety of attractive forms and colours, often with a sensuous velvety texture.

This exotic flower used to be the prerogative of the rich and was eagerly sought after by aristocratic collectors for their Orchid Houses. House guests would be presented with a corsage or table setting to brighten a drab winter's evening and this flower is particularly suitable for adding an exotic touch to winter celebration cakes.

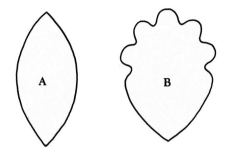

*1* Roll out and cut a petal shape from a sheet of flower paste using a cutter in the shape of **A**.

*2* Place the petal shape on a dry household sponge and then thin the edges by gentle pressure with a ball-shaped modelling tool.

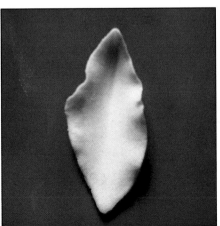

*3* Immediately mark petal with a cocktail stick along its centre.

*4* Gently insert 28 gauge green wire, moistened with egg white, through the petal's base for about ⅓ of the petal's length. 5 petals are required.

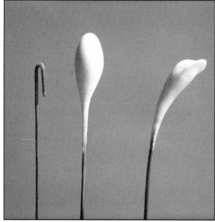

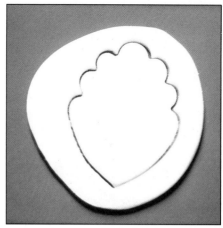

**5** (A) Cut and bend, to shape shown, a length of lime green 24 gauge wire.
(B) Mould a piece of flower paste to form a cone. Moisten end of wire and insert into cone and then mould base to the stem.
(C) Pinch one side of the cone to form the shape shown, which becomes the centre of the flower.

**6** With a cutter in the shape of **B** cut petal shape shown from a sheet of flower paste.

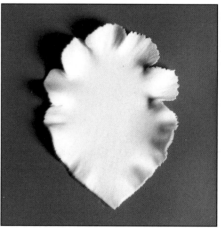

**7** Start to frill the edge of the petal by rolling a cocktail stick backwards and forwards.

**8** Complete the frilling of the petal, with emphasis on the top section.

**9** Moisten the centre of the petal and immediately fix the petal to the flower head.

**10** Bind together with floral tape three of the **B** petal shapes, leaving tape end as shown.

*11* Bind in two further petals as shown.

*12* Bend flower centre gently downwards until parallel with stem. Bind in to complete the flower. Flowers can be coloured with confectioners' dusting powder as shown below.

# Fuchsia

*T*he Fuchsia is a dramatic flower with bold colouring and a distinctive shape. A charming legend concerning the introduction of fuchsias to England tells that the sailor son of a humble widow living in Wapping brought home a fuchsia from South America to cheer up his ageing mother. Eventually the old lady was able to exchange it with a local nurseryman for three new plants and a great sum of money.

Fuchsias flower throughout the spring and summer and are most suitable for cake designs which require flashes of brilliant colour.

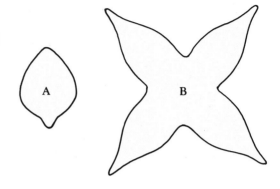

**1** (A) Cut and bend a length of lime green 24 gauge wire to form a small hook. Loop eight single stamens through the hook and twist the wire stem to secure them. (B) Cut off heads of one end. Turn stamen heads to upright position. Tape stamen heads to the stem with floral tape.

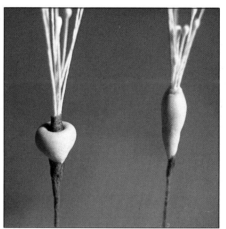

**2** (A) Mould a cone of flower paste. Moisten the tape at the base of stamens with egg white and insert the stem through the flower paste ball, as shown. (B) Mould base of cone into shape as shown.

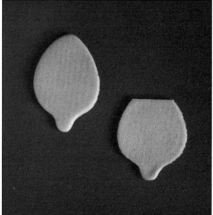

**3** With a cutter in the shape of **A**, cut a petal from a sheet of flower paste. Trim off the top section of the petal as shown.

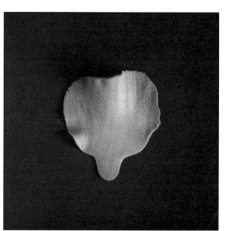

**4** Place the shape on a dry household sponge and thin the edge by gentle pressure with a ball-shaped tool. Remove from sponge. Frill the edge of the petal by rolling a cocktail stick backwards and forwards.

**5** Moisten the centre of the petal and immediately fix the petal to the flower head.

**6** Repeat steps **3-4** to make another petal. Turn flower head and add moistened petal as shown.

**7** Add two further petals to form bell-shaped flower centre. Allow to dry for 24 hours.

**8** Using a clean, soft artists' brush, colour the flower petals with confectioners' dusting powder.

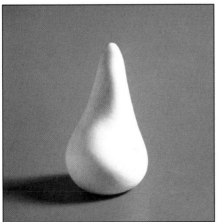

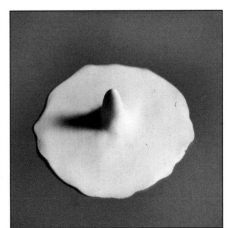

**9** Form a cone from flower paste.

**10** Place on a clean household sponge and gently flatten the edge using a ball-shaped modelling tool, leaving a protruding cone in the centre as shown.

*11* Using a cutter in the shape of **B**, carefully cut sepals ensuring that the cone is in the centre.

*12* Turn shape over and make a central hole with a suitable tool. Moisten centre.

*13* Insert wire of flower through the hole in the sepal.

*14* Mould cone to wire stem.

*15* Gently curl sepals down into shape shown.

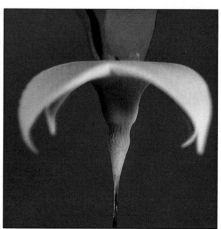

*16* Using a clean, fine artists' brush colour with green confectioners' dusting powder round the base of the flower where it joins the stem.

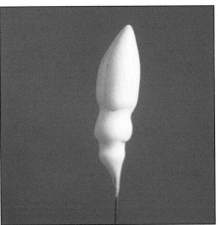

*17* Fuchsia buds can be made from a cone of flower paste moulded onto moistened 28 gauge wire. Form shape shown and then mark top with a cocktail stick to indicate petals.

*18* Using a clean, fine artists' brush colour the base of the bud with green confectioners' dusting powder.

# Cattleya

*T*he exotic Cattleya takes its name from an amateur grower, William Cattley. In the early nineteenth century he took a keen interest in the flower and when he died his collection passed to a firm of nurserymen who became orchid specialists. There are now over sixty species of Cattleyas which originated in the jungles of Central and South America and the West Indies.

In the language of flowers the magnificent Cattleya declares "I await your favours" and this flower is suitable for decorating cakes during any season.

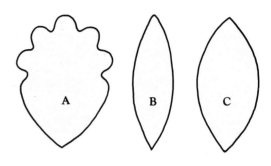

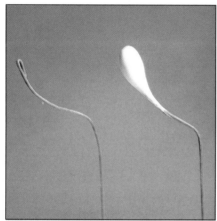

**1** (A) Cut and bend to shape shown a length of 24 gauge lime green wire. (B) Mould a piece of flower paste to form a cone. Moisten end of wire with egg white and insert into cone and then mould base of the cone to the stem.

**2** (A) Pinch top of cone to give a 'peaked cap' effect. (B) Pinch both sides of the cone, below the peak, to form two 'ears'. This forms the flower's tongue.

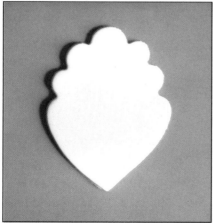

**3** With a cutter in the shape of **A**, cut petal shape from a sheet of flower paste.

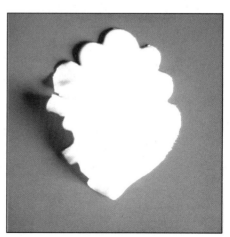

**4** Start to frill the edge of the petal, rolling a cocktail stick backwards and forwards along the outer edge.

**5** Continue frilling the edge to create a pronounced frill, particularly around the top of the petal.

**6** Moisten the base of the frill and fold it around the flower tongue, keeping the pinched sides facing the petal. This forms the throat. Leave to dry for 1 hour.

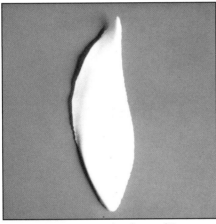

**7** With a cutter in the shape of **B**, cut a petal from a sheet of flower paste. Using finger and thumb, sharpen each edge as shown.

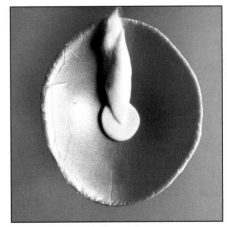

**8** Place a small disc of flower paste in the centre of a shallow dish (the one illustrated was cut from an apple tray). Moisten the centre and fix petal as shown.

**9** Make and fix two further petals as shown.

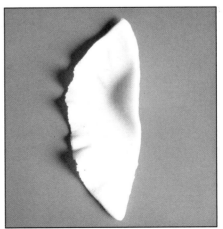

**10** With a cutter in the shape of **C**, cut two petals. Gently frill the edges of each petal using a cocktail stick.

*11* Fix the petals in place as shown. Pierce a hole in the centre through the flower and the dish.

*12* Moisten the centre of the petals. Insert the wire of the flower throat through the hole so that the throat sits firmly in the centre. Leave to dry 1 hour. Colour with confectioners' dusting powder.

# Azalea

*T*he brilliantly coloured flame, orange, apricot, pink and scarlet flowers of the Azalea make a striking decoration for celebration cakes of all kinds.

Many of these wonderful colours were first grown in Europe by a baker who lived in Ghent in the early 1800s and who combined together species from North America and Asia Minor to form the magnificent hybrids available today.

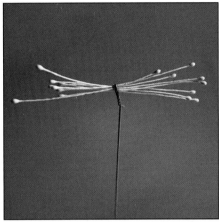

*1* Bind together eight single stamens at different distances (as illustrated) with a piece of 24 gauge wire twisted around the middle.

*2* (A) Cut the heads off one side of the stamens and then turn into an upright position as shown. (B) Bind together with floral tape to make a firm stem.

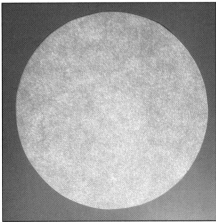

*3* Cut a disc of grease-proof paper 100mm (4″) in diameter.

*4* Fold the disc into a cone shape as shown and secure with sticky tape.

5 Using a cutter in the shape of **B**, cut from flower paste the shape shown to form the calyx.

6 Smooth the edges of the calyx between finger and thumb and then place in the centre of the greaseproof paper cone.

7 With a cutter in the shape of **A**, cut a petal from flower paste.

8 Frill the edge of the petal by rolling a cocktail stick backwards and forwards. Leave the base of the petal untouched.

9 Continue to frill the petal over the top and three-quarters of the way down the side as shown.

10 Place petal on to a dry household sponge and mark the 'veins' using the point of a cocktail stick, working down from the petal tip to the base.

*11* Moisten the base of the petal with egg white and fix to the calyx.

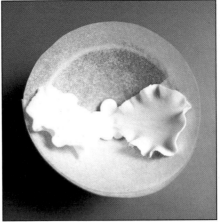

*12* Repeat steps *7-10*, then fix that petal opposite the first petal.

*13* Repeat steps *7-10* for a further two petals and fix into the formation shown, overlapping the petals as necessary.

*14* Repeat steps *7-10* then fix the last petal as shown. Make a hole at the centre, piercing through the greaseproof paper at the same time.

*15* Push the wired stem through the central hole and secure with a small piece of moistened flower paste.

*16* Moisten and fix flower paste at the base of the flower to the stem. Wrap the base and stem with floral tape. Dust the underneath of the flower and base with confectioners' dusting powder.

*17* Dust the top-side of each petal with confectioners' dusting powder, highlighting the outer edges.

*18* Paint spots on the inside of the petals as shown. The spots should be close together at the centre, thinning out towards the edges. Bind single flowers together to form a cluster.

# Daisy

There are several varieties of Daisy, many having unusual colouring. The Rain Daisy has golden centered, glistening white flowers with a mauve ring around the centre and a delicate mauve back to the petals. The Ox-Eye Daisy used to be called the Moon Daisy because its large white petals shone like the full moon. The delightfully named Hen & Chickens produces small clusters of 'children' around the 'parent flower'.

In Scotland the Daisy is called the Bairnwort, 'the children's flower', and children everywhere still gather Daisies for Daisy chains. This flower makes a delightful decoration for children's cakes.

*1* Using a cutter in the shape of **A**, cut petals from a thinly rolled sheet of flower paste.

*2* Using a clean, sharp knife, cut each petal along its length and separate to create twice the number of petals.

*3* Roll a cocktail stick at the centre of each petal to produce an upturned, curved shape as shown.

*4* Place the petal shape into a shallow dish (the one shown was cut from an apple tray).

**5** Repeat steps **1-3**. Moisten the centre of the petal shape in the dish and fix the second petal shape on to the first. Pierce a hole through the centre of the flower and dish.

**6** Turn the end of a piece of 24 gauge wire into a small circle. Guide the wire through the hole, from the front, and fix into position with moistened flower paste.

**7** Roll out a small ball of flower paste and flatten slightly to form a dome.

**8** Press a square of tulle over the dome so that the flower paste is marked into stamens. Gently peel off the tulle in one continuous movement.

**9** Moisten the back of the flower paste, and carefully position in the centre of the daisy petals. Press the outer edge of the stamens with a cocktail stick to secure.

**10** Using cutters in the shape of **B** and **C**, cut two pieces of green flower paste to make calyxes.

**11** Remove the daisy from the dish. Moisten the shape from cutter **B** and fix to the back of the daisy after inserting the stem through its centre.

**12** Using cutter in the shape of **B**, repeat steps *2-4* and *6-9* to make a smaller daisy. Use shape **C** for the calyx. Colour the daisies with confectioners' dusting powder as required.

# Carnation

According to legend the Carnation sprang into being from the tears shed by the Virgin Mary on her way to Calvary, and the Pink Carnation is the emblem of Mother's Day, symbolising Mother Love. The Red Carnation signifies admiration and the White a pure and ardent love.

The Carnation is particularly suitable for Mother's Day cakes and can be matched to the colours of the flowers in the bridal bouquet for wedding cakes.

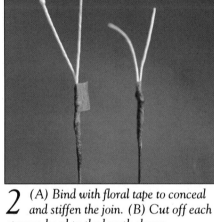

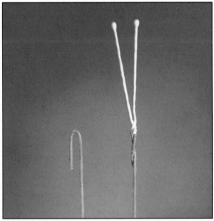

1 (A) Cut, and bend to the shape shown, a length of green 24 gauge wire to form the stem. (B) Loop a double headed stamen wire through the wire hook and secure by twisting the stem.

3 Using a cutter in the shape of **A**, cut petal shape from a thinly rolled sheet of flower paste.

2 (A) Bind with floral tape to conceal and stiffen the join. (B) Cut off each stamen head to the length shown.

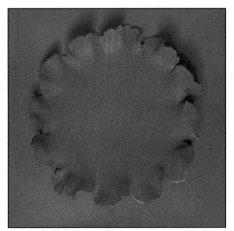

4 Immediately frill the petal shape by gently rolling a cocktail stick backwards and forwards on the crimped edge.

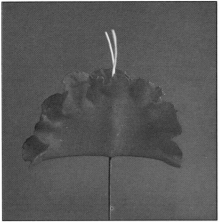

5 Moisten the centre of the petal shape with egg white. Push the stem through the centre and gently pull until the stamens protrude above the petal. Fold petal shape as shown.

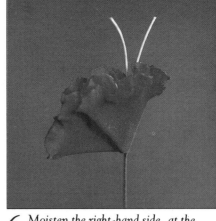

6 Moisten the right-hand side, at the base of the flower head, and fold over as shown, gently pressing to secure.

7 Turn the flower over and moisten the right-hand side at the base of the flower-head. Gently fold over and press to secure. This forms the centre of the carnation.

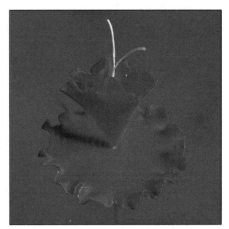

8 Repeat steps 3 and 4. Moisten the centre of the petal shape and push the flower stem through the centre.

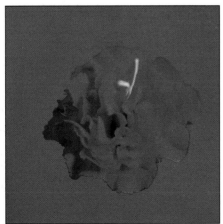

9 Wrap the petal shape around the flower head, using finger tips to splay out the petals as shown. Repeat steps 8 and 9. Additional petal shapes can be added if required. Leave to dry for 24 hours.

10 Mould a piece of flower paste to form a cone shape with flattened edges. Using a cutter in the shape of **B** carefully cut sepals (see steps *1-4*, page 80). Moisten and fix to base of flower.

*11* Using a cutter in the shape of **C** cut out the calyx from flower paste. Moisten the top and push the stem through the centre of the calyx.

*12* Fold the calyx up into position to form a bulbous base tapering off at the stem. Leaving short lengths free, wrap floral tape around the stem and cut the ends to form leaves as shown below.

# Primrose

*T*he Primrose was the favourite flower of Disraeli, the Victorian Prime Minister, and the Primrose featured in many old recipes of the time. A particular favourite was 'Primrose Pudding', a delectable confection of the petals boiled in milk, almonds, honey and ginger.

In the language of flowers this flower symbolises early youth and young love which makes it particularly suitable for cakes celebrating a teenage birthday or engagement.

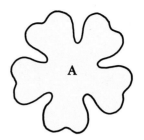

*1* Using a cutter in the shape of **A**, cut the five-petalled primrose head from thinly rolled flower paste.

*2* Roll a cocktail stick backwards and forwards over each petal. Do not flute the edge too much, and allow the petals to curl naturally.

*3* Continue thinning each petal to about twice its original size, letting the petals overlap as necessary.

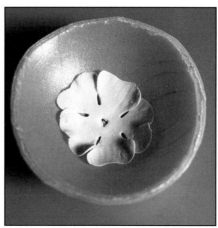

*4* Place the flower head into a shallow dish (the one illustrated was cut from an apple tray) and pierce a hole through the flower centre and the dish.

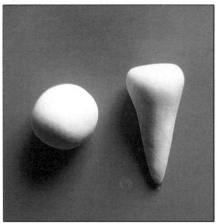

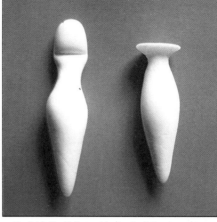

5 (A) Mould a piece of flower paste into a ball. (B) Roll the ball into a cone shape as shown.

6 (A) Roll the wide end of the cone into the shape shown and cut off the surplus. (B) Pinch the cut end between finger and thumb to form the vase shape. This is the base of the flower.

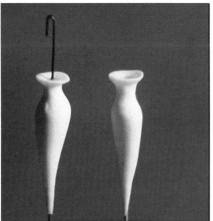

7 (A) Bend over the end of a piece of 24 gauge wire and insert the other end into the base of the flower. (B) Moisten the wire stem and continue pushing it into the base until concealed. Mould the bottom of the base to the wire to fix securely.

8 Moisten the top of the flower base and fix the flower head to it. Leave to dry 1 hour.

9 Brush confectioners' dusting powder over the flower head to achieve the depth of colour required.

10 Brush confectioners' dusting powder mixed with clear alcohol over the centre of the flower head to produce a deeper colour.

**11** Brush green confectioners' dusting powder mixed with clear alcohol in to the hole at the flower centre.

**12** Colour the base and underneath of the flower with confectioners' dusting powder.

# Daphne

D*aphne is a delicate, fragrant flower which is used for Oriental perfumes. The colour of Daphne can range from creamy white to greenish yellow, from palest pink or lilac through rose pink to deep purplish red and it is usually accompanied by glossy, deep green leaves.*

*It is an early flowering shrub and is particularly useful for February cakes.*

**1** (A) Roll flower paste into a ball.
(B) Mould the ball into the cone shape shown.

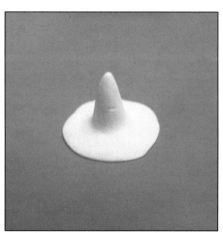

**2** Keeping the cone upright, press out the flower paste to form a large base.

**3** Using the cutter shape shown, carefully place the cutter over the cone and cut the base to form the petals.

**4** Press the edge of each petal between the finger and thumb to sharpen and curl into the required shape.

**5** Bend the end of a piece of 28 gauge wire and insert it into the centre of the daphne as shown. Moisten wire to secure in position.

**6** Pipe dots for the stamens and colour with confectioners' dusting powder. The shape of the daphne can be varied by raising or lowering the petals slightly.

# Unwired Open Rose

Roses are ideal decoration for a wedding cake as the association between the Rose and the marriage ceremony is a very ancient one. Crowns of roses used to be placed on the heads of brides and rose petals were thrown over the couple afterwards. As rose petals were hard to come by in the winter, eventually the rose petals were replaced by the much less romantic confetti. Bridal bouquets however still continue the tradition of having this beautiful flower at the wedding.

Gathering Roses in a dream signifies great joy whilst receiving Roses indicates that you are well and truly loved.

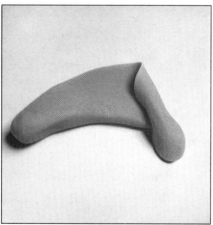

*1* Mould a piece of flower paste into a long roll, which tapers off one side, as shown.

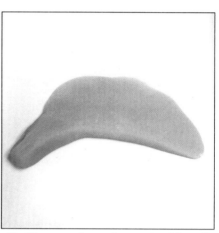

*2* Flatten and spread one side of the roll to produce a sharp edge.

*3* Beginning with the thinnest end, tightly roll the paste from right to left.

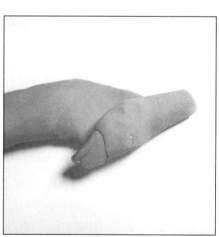

*4* Continue to roll the paste, turning the base across the main lie of the roll.

**5** Cut and remove the unwanted paste from the base. Shape the end of the bud between the finger and thumb. Curl back the open, outer side of the petal to complete the bud shape. Leave to dry 24 hours.

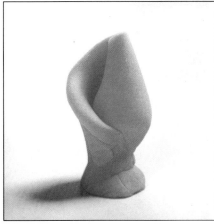

**6** Repeat steps **1-4**. Cut and remove the unwanted paste from the base. Flatten the base and place the bud in an upright position as shown.

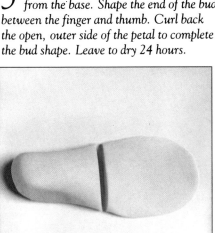

**7** Roll out a piece of paste, flatten one end to form a thin petal. Cut the petal off as shown.

**8** Moisten the centre of the petal with egg white and wrap it around the upright bud. Repeat steps **7-8** until the shape shown is achieved.

**9** Continue to make and fix further petals, gently curving each one outwards as it is fixed in position.

**10** Allow to dry as necessary to avoid the petals collapsing, and continue to add further petals, gradually increasing petal size, until the rose is complete.

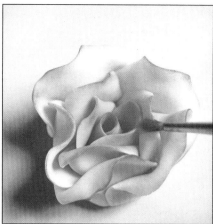

**11** Brush confectioners' dusting powder over the edge of each petal to the strength of colour required for the rose.

**12** Make and fix a paste calyx and base (see pages 75-76) to the rosebud and colour as desired.

# Decorated Vase

A decorated vase can look very attractive as the centrepiece of a cake, or as a table decoration. The vase illustrated is filled with Roses, Freesias and Daphnes.

The flowers should be made in advance and allowed to dry thoroughly.

*1*   *Fill the vase with sugar paste and add ribbon loops and trailing stems.*

*2*   *Place larger blossoms around the top edge of the vase and gradually fill-in and build up the centre with blossom and buds, creating a rounded shape which can be viewed from any angle.*

**ITEMS REQUIRED FOR VASE ILLUSTRATED**

○ 8 Roses

○ 5 Freesia sprigs

○ 8 Daphne

○ Ribbon loops

NOTE: *Freesias can be made in a similar manner to steps* **1-8** *of the Fuchsia flower (pages 60-61), coloured as appropriate. (The stamens should not protrude above the petals.) Buds can be formed from sugarpaste using steps* **1** *and* **2 (a)**, *page 54. The calyx of the bud should be painted on using a fine paintbrush and edible food colouring.*

# Catkin

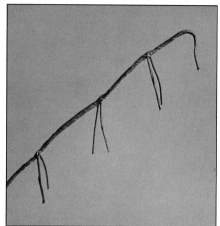

**1** To a length of 24 gauge wire, tape together short lengths of 28 gauge wire folded over to form pairs of hanging wires as shown. Bend the top end of the branch over to the shape shown.

**2** Pipe pointed dots with royal icing on each hanging wire, completely covering the surface, to form a catkin (MF 2). Leave to dry for 1 hour.

# Heather

1 *Tape together lengths of 28 gauge wire to form a main stem. Bend out each wire from the stem and trim to form an uneven pattern as shown.*

2 *Pipe leaves and flower heads with royal icing on the stem and branches to create the effect shown (MF 1). Leave to dry for 1 hour.*

# Lily of the Valley

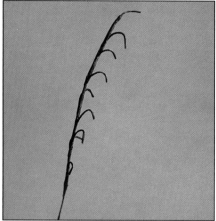

**1** Tape together short pieces of 28 gauge wire to a 24 gauge wire main stem. Bend each piece to a deep curve and position to one side of the main stem.

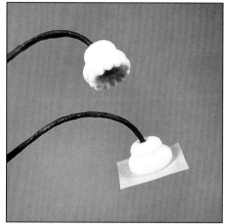

**2** Pipe a bell shape, with royal icing, on waxed paper and immediately push the bell onto the tip of a wire (MF 2). Repeat for each flower head. Leave to dry 12 hours. Remove waxed paper and pipe dots around each flower (MF 1). Leave to dry 2 hours.

# Pussy Willow

*1* Tape short lengths of 28 gauge wire to a 24 gauge wire stem. Trim each wire to make short stubs as shown.

*2* Pipe a bulb, with royal icing, on a stub (MF 2) and immediately pipe a calyx at the base of each bulb (MF 1). Repeat for each flower head. Leave to dry 2 hours.

# Viburnum

*1* Tape together five lengths of 28 gauge wire to a main stem of 24 gauge wire to form a circle of branches as shown.

*2* Pipe dots, with royal icing, around a branch top and then a dot at the centre to form a flower (MF 1). Repeat on each branch. Leave to dry 2 hours.

# Foliage

*1* Tape pieces of 28 gauge wire on to a 24 gauge wire stem. Bend to give an irregular shape and length to each branch.

*2* Pipe leaves, with royal icing, on to branches and stem, using a cut piping bag (see page 11). Leave to dry for 2 hours.

# Floral Spray

IN addition to being used as a decorative feature on a cake, floral sprays can be used to create unusual place and table settings, particularly in the winter time when fresh flowers are difficult to obtain.

The flowers should be made and allowed to dry thoroughly before taping up into a spray. Freesia flowers and buds with single Daphne were used to create the spray shown below.

Sprays can be used to decorate table napkins, candleholders and the knife for cutting the celebration cake. Co-ordinated colour schemes, with matching table linen, create an overall, harmonious appeal.

### ITEMS REQUIRED FOR THE SPRAY ILLUSTRATED
- ○ 3 Freesia blooms
- ○ 6 buds
- ○ 7 small Daphne
- ○ 2 sprigs
- ○ Ribbon loops

NOTE: *Freesias can be made in a similar manner to steps **1-8** of the Fuchsia flower (pages 60-61), coloured as appropriate. (The stamens should not protrude above the petals). Buds can be formed from sugarpaste using steps **1-2** (**a**) page 54. The calyx of the bud should be painted on using a fine paintbrush and edible food colouring.*

*1 Tape together four buds as shown.*

*2 Tape 2 open flowers and a ribbon loop to the main stem.*

*3 Tape 2 double ribbon loops below the flower head, as shown.*

*4 Tape 3 small flowers and one open flower just below the double ribbon loops.*

5 Tape a selection of ribbon loops, as shown, to the main stem.

6 Tape 4 small flowers around the main stem.

7 Using a wider ribbon than that used above, tape a pair of double ribbon loops to the main stem.

8 Tape a pair of triple ribbon loops to the stem, and then turn them to loop up neatly under the other loops.

9 Tape 4 small flowers and 2 buds to the main stem and gently ease up into position under the main spray.

10 Tape a sprig of buds and flowers to the main stem. Bend the sprig upwards in an 'S' shape.

**11** Tape a further sprig and bend to match the other side.

**12** Tape the base of the spray, securing all wires. Trim stem to length required using a strong pair of wire cutters.

# Floral Posy

FLORAL posies are seen at their best on a round cake with plenty of space around the posy.

As the posy shape is circular, round flowers are the easiest to work with. The flowers should be made in advance and allowed to dry thoroughly.

Carnations, Daphne and buds were used to create the posy illustrated below. Begin by taping together three stems of blossom and adding ribbon loops. Work in a circular fashion adding larger flowers, foliage and other blossom until the desired size is achieved. Finish with ribbon loops and wrap in lace. Tape the stems securely and fix into a posy holder.

# INDEX